P9-CFT-360

ALFRED A. KNOPF

1915 · 100 YEARS · 2015

The Players

The Players

Poems

JILL BIALOSKY

ALFRED A. KNOPF   NEW YORK   2015

THIS IS A BORZOI BOOK
PUBLISHED BY ALFRED A. KNOPF

Copyright © 2015 by Jill Bialosky

Published in the United States by Alfred A. Knopf,
a division of Random House LLC, New York, and
distributed in Canada by Random House of Canada Limited,
Toronto, Penguin Random House companies.

www.aaknopf.com/poetry

Knopf, Borzoi Books, and the colophon are
registered trademarks of Random House LLC.

Library of Congress Cataloging-in-Publication Data
Bialosky, Jill.
[Poems. Selections]
The players : poems / by Jill Bialosky.—First edition.
pages ; cm
"This is a Borzoi Book"—Title page verso.
Includes bibliographical references.
ISBN 978-0-385-35262-8 (hardcover)—ISBN 978-0-385-35263-5 (eBook)
I. Title.
PS3552.I19A6   2015
811'.54—dc23   2014013600

Front-of-jacket photograph courtesy of the Dana family
Jacket design by Oliver Munday

Manufactured in the United States of America
First Edition

For L.M.S.

Contents

American Comedy

Interlude

The Players

The Players

The Lucky Ones

Our labor realized in the crowns
of marigolds, blue eyes of the hydrangeas,
smell of lavender and late bloom of the hosta's
erect purple flower with its marvel of thick
green leaves. In our twilight
every year we trimmed back and the garden grew
more lustrous and untamable as if the eternal woods
and animals asleep at night in its beds were claiming it back.
The water in the pool shimmered an icy Tuscan blue.

When we arrived we swam
until the stress from the grueling
life in the city released our bodies. Later
we sat under the umbrella and watched a garter snake
slip into the water, careful not to startle
its flight-or-fight response. Its barbed-wire
coil. Comet of danger, serpent of the water,
how long we had thwarted the venom of its secret
lures and seductions.
It swam by arching then releasing
its slithery mercurial form.
Through the lanky trees
we heard the excited cries

of the neighbor's children—ours, the boy of our late youth,
of our happiness and our struggles, the boy who made us whole
and broken, was in his room perhaps dreaming
of a girl and sleeping the long, tangled sleep of a teenager.

It was a miracle, our ignorance. It was grace
incarnate, how we never knew.

Manhood

1. Chatter

Turn two. Balk. Way to hump.
Hey now, kid, hey now.
Good eye. That's all right.
That's all right. Good cut.
Inside. Watch the batter.
Hey way to drop it in there, kid.
That's the way to hop. Let's go.
Throw the baseball now. Heads up.
Dig, dig, dig. Batter's safe.
We got him in a pickle. He's out.
Look at that chug-o-lug.
Good scoop. Next one's coming.
Going. Good rip. Stretch that.
Go two, go two. Now we got three.

2. Manhood

If I say slide, get dirty.
If I say stay, don't run.
Two dead. Make it three.
Let's go, kid.
Good idea.
Take it for the team.
It's raining.
The smell is mint and grass,
dust and dirt
and the deeper odor
of the body.
The boy goes for the catch,
slips and falls.
We don't slow down.
We don't slow down.
Wipe it off your face
and shrug it off.
Win the battle.
Get mean.

3. The Hotdog

Watch him flip
them the bird
after the ball
comes flying,
a line drive hit hard
between first and second
just outside his reach,
he dives for it,
catches it,
and lobs it to first.
Years of practice,
mornings up
before dawn,
long afternoons
cascading into dusk—
no one can touch him.
Out on the field,
under the commanding
sun he's claimed his position.
He is old enough
to know his story
is no longer his coach's

nor his father's.
When the outfield retires,
and he takes the plate,
look. Watch him
pound it out of the park.

4. The Pack

Like wolves
who rely on scent markings
to define and mark
territory, they mentally
define their space.
They know exactly
what patch of ground
is theirs to protect,
how far they'll have to stretch,
slide, pull back, or lean in.
Sometimes they get down
on their haunches,
dig in their cleats,
pound their fists
in their mitt, to stave
off their opponent.
Their eyes widen
at every movement.
Sometimes they have to circle
each other, be back up,
take one out to save the pack.
They know each other's strengths
and weaknesses.
Their odor is fierce and feral.

5. Mind Game

It was a thinking game.
You had to know the rules
and the plays.
You had to know them so well
you could do them in your sleep.
And sometimes in your sleep
it was all you could think of.
What to do if men were on second
and third and offense bunts to first.
Which guy do you throw out?
The thinking came in handy.
You had to not always
think with your balls,
the Dominican coach had warned.
Use your goddamn cabeza.
You knew not to laugh
when the coach was angry.
It was a head game
and sometimes the head
got fucked up and you were off
your game for weeks.
Hit like a girl. Speaking of which,
the rules applied there too.

Know when to step back
and you had the ball
right in your hand.
It was like the sound
of the wind through the trees,
her hair caressing your face
when she leaned in.
You had to think with your body
so that soon you were not thinking at all.
Soon something had taken hold
and it was as though another
more enlightened being emerged
and you knew exactly what
you were doing without thinking.
The feeling was light as air, quick, confident.
It was like having the girl right there
beside you. There was nothing better
than the adrenaline rush
when you knew you'd beat out
the batter, when you snapped
that ball and threw
and it landed straight
in the other player's mitt.
And the player was called out.
And through the diamond grille
in the fence your eye caught hers
and your body exploded into bliss.

6. The Girls

The day the boys played us
it was not in our beds
or in the backseat
of a car or in a field
on a blanket.
They played us
with the magnificence
of their bodies.
They did not know
that when we watched
them make a play with skill
and grace like chess masters
advancing pieces
on a board—silent
guardians of their own
sacred positions—
they had us.
Their bodies
were like fortresses,
their minds
half-barred windows.
They played us with intensity.
They played us

eager and as they played us
we knew we were different.
What we liked most
was their strength,
the throbbing
muscles in their necks,
the way their callused
hands gripped
the bat, ready to bear down,
ready to get some.
They did not know
it was enough
to find us with their eyes
across the field
behind the gated fence
when the air smelled
of manure and rotting grass
when we did not yet
know we wanted them.

7. Brothers

Remember when you called Bixby ugly?
You told him to shut his face.
You shouldn't've done that, man.
You're right. Shouldn't've.
There's our boy.
He's coming in to lead the pack.
He looks good out there.
How much you want to bet
he coughs up his chicken.
We shouldn't've eaten all that shit.
We had three donuts each.
Tomorrow we go healthy.
That movie scared the crap out of me.
Mr. I go call Mommy after *Ghost Hunters*.
I just wanted to hear her voice.
That's the girl
I was telling you about.
I just liked what she said
commenting on her status.
I don't know what else to say.
No man, I don't even know her.
Did you see her status?
You're a relationship man.

You're going to marry a redhead.
She's not going to be a burden.
She's not one of those girls.
Poor Bixby. His teeth are in bad shape too.
Don't rip on Bixby.
Remember when he passed out?
That kid almost died.
I'm worried about my old man.
He's going to the Giants game on 9/11.
You think they'd blow up a stadium?
Yeah. Maybe I am a better son.
Lots of fathers and sons get emotional.
Not mine. If I don't call him, he don't call me.
I text my old man every morning.
You and your dad have balance.
Like I said, you guys got balance.
If I tell you everything,
how am I going to stay ahead of you?
Did you see that Underarm?
It's sick. I'm going to get me one of those.
If you can survive Economics
you should take Business,
everything goes back to Business.
Our boy sure looks pretty out there.
Did you see his footwork?
Did you see that slide?

8. The Mothers

We loved them.
We got up early
to toast their bagels.
Wrapped them in foil.
We filled their water bottles
and canteens. We washed
and bleached their uniforms,
the mud and dirt
and blood washed clean
of brutality. We marveled
at their bodies,
thighs thick as the trunk
of a spindle pine,
shoulders broad and able,
the way their arms filled out.
The milk they drank.
At the plate we could make out
their particular stance, though each
wore the same uniform as if they were
cadets training for war.
If by chance one looked up at us
and gave us a rise with his chin,
or lifted a hand, we beamed.

We had grown used to their grunts,
mumbles, and refusal to form a full sentence.
We made their beds and rifled through their pockets
and smelled their shirts to see if they were clean.
How else would we know them?
We tried to not ask too many questions
and not to overpraise.
Sometimes they were ashamed of us;
if we laughed too loud,
if one of us talked too long to their friend,
of our faces that had grown coarser.
Can't you put on lipstick?
We let them roll their eyes,
curse, and grumble at us
after a game if they'd missed a play
or lost. We knew to keep quiet;
the car silent the entire ride home.
What they were to us was inexplicable.
Late at night, after they were home in their beds,
we sat by the window and wondered
when they would leave us
and who they would become
when they left the cocoon of our instruction.
What kind of girl they liked.
We sat in a group and drank our coffee
and prayed that they'd get a hit.
If they fumbled a ball or struck out

we felt sour in the pit of our stomach.
We paced. We couldn't sit still or talk.
Throughout summer we watched
the trees behind the field grow fuller
and more vibrant and each fall
slowly lose their foliage—
it was as if we wanted to hold on
to every and each leaf.

9. The Fathers

While we waited in our cars,
already gassed up, still dawn,
no light, dark as a motherfucker,
they got up late, slunk out of bed
and into the shower, and took too
long under the water.
We waited for them to stumble out the door,
crawl into the back, and stretch out,
their hair still wet,
and sleep again while we drove
sometimes two hours to the field.
When they woke we gave them
bacon-and-egg sandwiches.
We wanted them to get stronger, meaner.
We wanted their bodies to perform
like well-oiled machines.
We'd been there before.
We worked, some of us at jobs we didn't like,
in offices, in hospitals, in construction,
to put food on the table and make the mortgage,
to send our boys to college.
In our offices we pushed aside documents
to make out rosters.
We evaluated their stance.
What they needed to do

to get underneath it,
to throw farther,
increase their speed,
realize their potential.
For years, after dinner, weekends,
we took them to the field
and threw the ball. Hit them grounders,
brought them to the cages.
When they hit the ball hard,
stole home, executed a double play,
we lived on it for days.
Some nights when they were in a slump
our dreams were inchoate and thick.
When they went up to bat we saw
if they'd partied too hard the night before.
One of us had a boy gone soft
for a girl and lost his focus.
Others had boys who were loud and cocky,
or meandered to the plate with heads bowed
as if they were living ghosts.
We saw when they were confident.
When they lacked drive.
Were defeated.
We paced.
We rattled the fence, cursed.
We scrutinized every play, unable to step

back, as if we were under a trance,
in some kind of white haze,
as if we were Abraham
under the instruction
of a benevolent God,
taking our son to the top
of the mount to sacrifice
his life for something
better than his forebearer.

10. The Spectators

Bold, brash, and obsessed,
for hours each day
they lift, go to the cages
swing the bat.
Clear-eyed,
single-minded, they
can't see anything beyond.
The outliers are scrappy,
unafraid to get dirty;
they slide and lunge.
They're the procrastinators,
the ones that barely work out,
like to have fun.
The timid ones are spindly,
they know they don't quite belong,
but tough it out.
The jokesters are perpetually late.
They send out texts before the game:
out still six in the morning, still drunk,
I'm fucked. There's at least one
on a team who thinks too hard.
He's analyzed speed, velocity,
knows how to read a ball.

For him nothing comes easy.
And look, farther afield comes
the soulful one still in half uniform,
soon to take the baton.

11. The Pillage

Time passes
into the limbs of the boys
on the field stretching
before the season's last game,
into memories of their phantom selves
tugging wheelbarrows
through fields, flying
gleefully over one bump
and another.
Into the lines
and furrows of their brows,
into the solid precision of their bodies
trained to field and battle,
time passes, the day nearly recollection.
They come rushing from the dugout
in uniform to take their positions,
confident, aware of the fleeting
glory of the moment,
their faces glow
like the last lightning bugs
of the season, heat and adrenaline
bursting from their bodies.
Let's watch the enlightened leaves burn
into dark and angry flames.

12. The Dugout

They like it here
shaded from the sun, drinking Gatorade
in the dugout among the solitude
of brothers.

After one strikes out
or misses a ball,
angry fathers climb the gated fence
that separates spectators
from players and curse.
All night only the male crickets chirp,

nocturnal and cold-blooded.
They take on the temperature
of their surroundings.
They run the top of one wing
along the teeth
at the bottom of the other.

Their wings up and open
like acoustical sails, the sound relentless
and unending.

13. The Players

Thirsty, hot, crazed
by the mosquitoes,
they've had enough.

At the plate,
they dig their cleats
into the batter's box.

Swing and miss.
Looks like a no-hitter,
the coach hisses.

The sunflowers grown gawky
behind the stands have matured
into a tougher flower.

The day darkens.
The season is finished.
They take off their caps.

American Comedy

American Comedy

They are tearing up fields where horses graze
for designer mansions. Cutting limbs off
trees, giving the grass severe manicures.
What's wrong with worry lines around the eyes?
The occasional gray hair? I'm tired
of exercise. It makes my spirit founder:
the persistent need for self-improvement.
I miss wildflowers, horse dung, and clover.
We've sacrificed quiet and contemplation
for the razzmatazz of conversation.
We favor reality over art;
pain medication for a broken heart.
I prefer decrepitude, even madness,
for sweet torture that precedes transcendence.

Sonnet for the Misbegotten

The surfers are on deck in black diving
penguin suits, fins on their feet—surfer school
for the youth of the rich set—determined
to catch a wave while somewhere less pristine,
another suffers from inner unrest.
Look, the anorexics are frantically
speed-walking the beach pumping three-pound weights,
ignoring the scenic ocean view.
At last evening's barbecue we discussed
our boys: dyslexic, attention deficient,
prone to depression. How will we get through?
A sandpiper, regal in white and gray,
pecking frantically in the sand, observes me,
creature from another world, on my deck chair.

American Pastoral

Say good-bye to black-eyed Susans, long sea
grasses. Late evening barbecues, children
digging in the sand, the praying mantis.
Put away your binoculars. Even
the birds are hiding for a better
season. One of us joined a support group
or is leaving the marriage. Another
needs to change meds. Teenagers are virtual-
dating. No need for soliloquy. We've
mastered the grand art of text. I'm sorry
the beloved beach house foreclosed. No matter.
Soon we'll gather in darkness. Kiss. Pour over-
zealous goblets. Later the children will
mock us. Someone will want to play charades.

Ode

Somebody stole my yellow flip-flops. I
guess they needed them more than me. I left
them by the side of the sand hill before
my beach walk. Everyone does. I bought them
at Kmart for ten ninety-nine. I wear
them in the garden cloud or shine. When I
am painting my toes. After my shower
they wait like a faithful friend so I don't
slip. They're the cheapest thing I own. It makes
me sad. The lack of humanity. The
guts. The betrayal. I searched the beach for
the culprit. A man with son digging a
castle. Another headed for a swim.
I regret I'll never see them again.

Coming Upon a Crab in the Sand

A sand crab has come loose from its hard shell,
thrown to shore by dangerous turbulence.
It lies sprawled on its back kicking its legs
like a baby awakening in a crib
when simply the sight of his mother's face
brings jubilation. I hope it is not
in agony. Now love morphs into some-
thing deep, intangible, rich, strange. What may
ink character? Devise soul? The brilliant
sun passes behind the nascent face of an
amorphous cloud and everything darkens.
A cornucopia of fears, rage, and
desire we don't know. The children
are growing up. It's time to let them go.

After the Storm

The harsh sand stings. The salt air is bitter.
The sun makes everything sharp. I pick up
a seashell and it crumbles. My mother
is frail. She forgets. Everything is covered
with Post-its. *An enriched beginning, a*
new life, the lit espoused as if the past
washed away in a brutal wave and freed
her. Look, an aged sea turtle has left
its shell in the sand. The golden beach widens.
A generation of seabirds is dying.
We laid a grave of new sand to replace
what's lost, erected seawalls to forestall
erosion. The terrain is unsettled.
We can't save our beaches. Or anyone.
Gulls scavenge the plot: the ocean's embroiled.

Morning Nocturne

I am glad today is dark. No sun. Sky
ribboning with amorphous, complicated
layers. I prefer cumulus on my
morning beach run. What more can we worry
about? Our parents are getting older
and money is running out. The children
are leaving, the new roof is damaged by
rain and rot. I fear the thrashing of the sea
in its unrest, the unforgiving cricket.
But that's not it. The current is rising.
The dramas are playing out. Perhaps
it's better to be among these sandpipers
with quick feet dashing out of the surf than
a person who wishes to feel complete.

Elegy

When I learned my first love died it was as
if no years had passed instead of twenty-five:
the sea turtles slowly crawl in the sand.
The peepers are quiet. The ocean roars.
Waves crash. Sky rumbles. The seabirds rush past.
Do surfers drift from fear or circumstance?
Why do the waves unfurl in loneliness?
The sun today is bright; it makes sparkles
and reflections on the water. The salt
hurts. Bugs bite. I no longer want to be
taunted. So commanding is memory.
It creeps up and distorts. Twists us in knots.
Seeps inside. Why is the mind's turbulence
so difficult to harness and withstand?

Tree

Look at the solid tree dug into earth
through eternity grandly observing
the world from the perch of its highest bloom.
Would we not all desire to end our days
at this height, happy to sway, to bend
our branches in harmony? No longer
dependent upon this one or that?
What would it be like to be without thought?
To feel wind slash the throat? To be empty
of all memory? To be without love
or regret or ego? To never suffer
the grief of others? Or would our days be
long, nights restless with only a simple band
to mark the significance of our passage?

Marriage Nests

In the tree in the yard is a bird's nest.
Remnants of paper, grass, tangled bloodroots;
a courtship; an elaborate masterpiece
of brutal entanglement. For some species,
a shallow depression made in sand.
Years ago when nothing much was at stake
we held hands in the park. The solid un-
swerving way the world newly divided
opened a field of possibility.
The birds are skittish or in harmony.
They draw sustenance from close comfort.
One cannot exist without the other.
I hear him get up, the sound of heavy footsteps.
Birds call. A cry deeper than hurt or love.

A View Without Illusion

On the streets of the quiet hillside college,
Amish mothers and daughters dressed in dark
handmade cloaks and hats tie a taut rope
between two trees to hang their quilts and woven
baskets; jam jars, buckets of picked flowers
adorn cardboard tables. A beautiful
blue star catches the light and makes the quilt
Day-Glo. On the other side of the road,
a family in a Mercedes unloads.
On the wire hops a blue jay, then a
regal cardinal. How much does difference
matter? All mothers must watch their children
thrive and suffer. The Amish in horse-drawn
black carriages load up their wares and trot past.

Summer's End

Take one last glimpse amidst summer season's
slaughter: crabs and cavernous shells, white stones,
shards of jellyfish and broken sea horse,
an abandoned, half-torn volleyball net.
Curled in the sand, a pair of August lovers.
Quick, jump in for one last dangerous swim.
The cool sea rumbles. It's time to pack up
rusty beach chairs, fold the damp towels, tie
up the umbrella before the bats settle in.
Leash the dog. Deer have devoured every
last glorious flower. On the beach
is a ship of decaying logs and white
sheets flapping in the breeze. We're all pirates
plundering, unable to settle for what's left.

Interlude

An Early Education

The Portrait of a Lady leaned against
A Tale of Two Cities and *The House of Mirth.*
One remarked of the other's strength,
the choices we must make,
and the dangers of misperception.
It was *The Age of Innocence.*
In one room the *Little Women* pondered
The Stranger. They were not compatible.
It was a matter of philosophy.
But that did not mean they did not long
to test their *Sense and Sensibility,*
The Sound and the Fury in their souls, their
powers of *Persuasion.* They were shrewd
and not without *Pride and Prejudice.*
They were *The Americans.*
They refused to wear hearts on sleeves
when *The Red Badge of Courage* would do.
They were descendants of *Jane Eyre*
and her solitary constitution, *Tender Is the Night,*
soon to set off alone, with *Great Expectations,*
and if by chance they were more daring
than most, they would test their gifts
in the *Heart of Darkness.* They were not foolish

enough to expect *The Little Prince,*
A Farewell to Arms seemed rather masculine,
and they were too young to appreciate
a *Remembrance of Things Past,*
too ignorant to recognize how
the plight of one protagonist
would force them to test their own moral compass,
how *War and Peace* might confound them,
how an early education sought in the splendor of the shelves
was only *The Prelude, Sanctuary,*
Treasure Island for the *Long Day's Journey*
into Night and *The Odyssey* that awaited them.

Jane Austen

"A fine Sunday in Bath empties every house of its inhabitants, and all the world appears on such an occasion to walk about and tell their acquaintance what a charming day it is." —NORTHANGER ABBEY

I awoke from the tunnel
to the fields of yellow rape,
seventeenth-century buildings, and cobbled
streets as she would have seen them.
It was rainy; the rain came and went,
came and went so that you could not escape
its dampness. I understood the need for tea
and the luxury of crèmes and pasties
and why the ladies longed for a strong shoulder
to see them through the winter.
The seagulls cried overhead,
though there was no sea, only a muddy river
from Bath to Bristol. The scavengers
lived on the rooftops and if desperate
enough would swoop down and take
a sandwich from your hand.
I secured my room at the Royal Bath Hotel.
It was a hovel, really, with a carpet
as old as the early century.

Walking through the hotel,
I sensed something lurid
in the air, every eye upon me as if they knew
I was a foreigner in a strange land.
Over the bed, a burgundy bedspread
dusty and faded as vintage wine,
made me long for the bright color of red.
In the next room, sleepless, I heard
through thin walls the sounds
of an un-tender coupling.
I looked in the warped mirror
and found myself ugly
and when I turned from it,
could not escape the vision.
It lingered. The rain came and went,
came and went. I took an umbrella
and began my walk, hoping to come upon
her quarters. I passed the Roman Baths,
the statues not beautiful,
but puckered and fossilled
and the Pump Room where her protagonist,
other self, doppelgänger,
good, strong, loyal Catherine,
longing for companionship, fell
under the seduction of Isabella
and her reprehensible brother.

Even then her coming out
seemed less magisterial,
and Bath a representation of the emptiness
and evils of society where a woman's dowry
might confine her forever,
than a reprieve from country life.
I gave up my search.
Images were everywhere.
And my mind had been made up.
I perceived no romance
in the wind, no comfort in the hard
glances of strangers, girls with chipped nail polish,
lads unkempt as if there were no hope of glory.
The next morning I boarded the train
to the modern world and it wasn't until a sheet
of blue slipped out like a love letter
from its envelope of dark gray sky
that I knew the journey had ended
and, like Catherine, I was finally safe.

Portrait of a Lady

"She closed her eyes; he had not hurt her, it was only a touch that she had obeyed. But there was something in his face that she wished not to see." —THE PORTRAIT OF A LADY

It was Isabel Archer we returned to.
She was as vital to us as our mothers,
close to us as if we knew the smell, touch,
and sound of her; we felt as if she
inhabited our very being.
We admired her refusal to marry
the aristocrat—*do you think Lord Warburton
could make me any better than I am?*—
and her free spirit.
We held our breath when she fled to Europe
to find herself and later marry for art and beauty,
gasped when we discovered
the depth of Osmond's betrayal,
prayed when she returned home
she'd find in Caspar Goodwood—
even his name embodied his down-to-earth spirit—
what we were looking for.

What was a lady? The word itself
antiquated, too prissy and prim
for our mothers of the fifties.
We were their joy and burden,
spectators of their merry-go-round lives.
Sometimes when they took us to the beach,
to flee the scrutiny of husbands,
we saw them come to life
in a strange man's gaze.
We felt their pulse quicken at the ballet,
or an exhibit at the museum,
as if their dreams bloomed full
and evanescent under the spell of art
or in the solitude of a dark auditorium.

We pondered again and again
the violence and heat of that last kiss—
how can you help me?—
the paradox of responsibility and destiny,
even though we knew she was no different
from us, and our mothers,
that when we love we are never free.

The Players

The Guardians

All day we packed boxes.
We read birth and death certificates.
The yellowed telegrams that announced
our births, the cards of congratulations
and condolences, the deeds and debts,
love letters, valentines with a heart
ripped out, the obituaries.
We opened the divorce decree,
a terrible document of division and subtraction.
We leafed through scrapbooks:
corsages, matchbooks, programs to the ballet,
racetrack, theater—joy and frivolity
parceled in one volume—
painstakingly arranged, preserved
and pasted with crusted glue.
We sat in the room in which the beloved
had departed. We remembered her yellow hair
and her mind free of paradox.
We sat together side by side
on the empty floor and did not speak.
There were no words
between us other than the essence
of the words from the correspondences,
our inheritance—plain speak,
bereft of poetry.

Crime Scene

The girl's room was painted the color of crème de menthe.
The paint now chipped and peeling, the aroma of some
awful liquor lingered. It had been her choice.
Her bedspread hot Barbie pink—another consolation
to ease the new arrangement—once bunched
at the foot of an unmade bed,
was folded in the upper reaches of the closet.
If opened, out might fly her nightmares
enacted in the dark, the cats sleeping beside her,
—one could see the scratches they'd made
on the walls—her father had long deserted her—
the girl had thrashed. The myth unfolded
in the long uninhabited room.
She was strong. Sturdy. Unbreakable.
The bathroom was another scene altogether.
Curling iron, hair products, headbands and scrunchies,
barrettes in different sizes and colors,
old and gooey jars of Noxzema
inside the cabinet underneath the sink,
her combs and brushes that held her fine hair still in the drawer.
The hours she must have looked at herself
in the clear circle her palm had cleared of steam
in the now distorted mirror
striving to make sure the image
did not reflect any of it.

Moving Day

Generations of bees and wasps,
lifespans of grasshoppers, lost wings
of moths and butterflies curl and decompose.
The movers have arrived with trolleys
and cavernous truck, ransacking the house
of its possessions. The rain is vacant, morning
unresolved in the subdued, funereal skies.
Strong roots of buckeyes and evergreens—
weeping of nuts and mettle, berries, kernels
of acorns and twigs—bare down in the mausoleum
of pebbled earth and stone. Under
the shingled roof and beamed ceiling,
in rooms where sleepers
quarreled, mourned, twisted in fits
of forgiveness, the pillage has begun.
Five decades of newspaper cutouts,
receipts, wills, and testaments emptied from drawers,
stacks of read and still-to-be-read books,
raided from shelves.
The light on the wood gains focus.
The plaster crumbles.
The movers begin the procession.
The kitchen emptied
of its elongated maple table and sensible
high-backed chairs,

the living room of its couch
and impressionable cushions;
the walls stripped of their camouflage of paintings
and portraits sealed under glass
to preserve the contours of its inhabitants.
Down comes the canopy bed, distorted
mirrors, lamps, and dressing tables;
unhinged, the antique clock with its face
of Roman numerals whose ornate hands
have stopped in prayer.

April Mornings

Mornings our mother got up,
climbed down the stairs,
and put up water for tea.

We'd wake and hear the crying
of the kettle and slowly part
the curtain to the frozen lawn.

Still in bed,
afraid to meet
the dull and sad

pennies of her eyes,
body limp as a fevered
child's, and the sour smell

of last night's sex,
fearing the persistent
madness of our house,

we'd hear the awful creak
of the iron mail chute open,
then the slice

of the knife slit open
the envelopes
of debts unpaid.

The yellow crocuses
were still buried
in their tender winter beds.

Pilgrims

The sisters were guardians
of the unknown, bound to each other,
foreigners on a journey from spiritual wretchedness
to beatitude, forging their own formidable
plot in the land without men.
Like all pilgrims
they trudged on with the knowledge
that no matter how gutted
the road, how hot the sun or formidable
the load, how distant the holiest point
of the journey, it was only when they
returned home to claim their legacy
that the pilgrimage was over.
Around the long farm table
they divided the assets, decreed the power
of attorney, honored the empty place
at the head of the table
reserved for the lost patriarch.
He was a grand ghost, an ephemeral ideal—a god
of their own rectitude.
In the yard, the widow's formidable,
unattended garden.

Red Rover

We take our last walk.
Walls stripped of portraits,

warped mirrors, dressing tables,
and the grandfather clock

with its stoic face
and elaborate gentle fingers.

For years we struggled to break
free of the closeness of rooms,

the obligation of birth order,
the metaphysics that bind

one element to the other,
as if we were still wild girls

playing red rover in the garden,
breaking through a chain of linked hands.

Daylight Savings

There was the hour
when raging with fever
they thrashed. The hour
when they called out in fright.
The hour when they fell asleep
against our bodies, the hour
when without us they might die.
The hour before school
and the hour after.
The hour when we buttered their toast
and made them meals
from the four important food groups—
what else could we do to ensure they'd get strong and grow?
There was the hour when we were spectators
at a recital, baseball game,
when they debuted in the school play.
There was the silent hour in the car
when they were angry. The hour
when they broke curfew. The hour
when we waited for the turn of the lock
knowing they were safe and we could finally
close our eyes and sleep. The hour
when they were hurt

or betrayed and there was nothing we could do
to ease the pain.
There was the hour
when we stood by their bedsides with ginger-ale
or juice until the fever broke. The hour
when we lost our temper and the hour
we were filled with regret. The hour
when we slapped their cheeks and held
our hand in wonder.
The hour when we wished for more.
The hour when their tall and strong bodies,
their newly formed curves and angles in their faces
and Adam's apple surprised us—
who had they become?
Hours when we waited and waited.
When we rushed home from the office
or sat in their teacher's classroom
awaiting the report of where they stumbled
and where they excelled, the hours
when they were without us, the precious hour
we did not want to lose each year
even if it meant another hour of daylight.

Driving Lesson

He is listening to Beach 104
on the radio dial,
singing along with the rapper.
He's been waiting
for this day for a long time.
He turns up the music.
I turn it down.
We drive along the road.
Horse farm on the side of the street
where we encounter a field
of young English riders with crops
preparing to mount the hurdles.
It won't be easy.
On the other side the day camp
he returned to every summer: the children
playing manhunt in the garden.
The clouds in the sky are moving too fast.
The berth filled with trees is too wide.
I look at the speedometer.
I want him to slow down.
The thrashers in the branches are frantic.
There must be more to teach him.
Eyes on the road,

ready to accelerate,
he glances into the rearview mirror
to see what's behind,
changes lanes and careens
gracefully into his manhood.
When I turn to look
I see the pensive boy in the backseat
strapped in his seat belt
watching two red squirrels run up a tree
and back down.

Prophesy

We knew how it worked.
Our precursors warned us.
It would happen when they were teenagers.
Still we didn't believe it. Not our boys.
The first time we thought
that they were under the influence
of a drug, or a conniving friend or girl.
They looked right through us, no longer
willing to abide. It was as if another being
had taken over, scorching even their hair
a deeper shade, stealing their voice.
When we went to kiss them
their cheeks turned to stone,
and when they looked at us
it was with disdain instead of adoration.
The kinder and more loving
we'd been meant we'd have it worse.
It was as if they were suddenly warned
of a prophesy
that would bring tragedy and gloom
if they did not turn away; it was as if they'd been
deceived or deluded; it was as if they were
Oedipus discovering he'd married
his mother and took the pin from her
dress, yes her dress,

and stabbed himself in the eye.
We knew there was nothing we could do
but ride it out, that for some
it might take years of wandering and exile,
of restraint and turmoil
until they'd finally come back
as if to seek refuge
in a grove of gentle trees.

The Guardians: Last Notes

They have built barricades along the windows,
Huge unsafe staircases with ropes and ladders,
Unknown traps and decoys.
In the city a maze of opportunity.
Behind one door is debauchery.
Behind the other is virtue.
If you enter the second door you will be free.
If you enter the first you will never leave.
When I dream you have departed.
When I wake you are omnipresent as a dark and private god.
When I pray I close my eyes and follow your silent footsteps
Into a forest of untouched snow.
I have opened the door. Unlatched the windows.
I have emptied myself of obligation.
When we go we take one or two with us:
One or two.

Perspective

For two days it was cold and it rained
and we were dark and worried.
We imagined car accidents,
arrests, emergency rooms,
harm, and danger.
We watched them go.
Perhaps we were envious,
having partaken of excess
to feel the capacity of joy, the intensity
of sex, liberation from constraint,
the sheer beauty of our beings
in full and splendid throttle.
We watched them go.
We imagined lives hindered
by calamity, of never
knowing or finding meaning.
For two days it was cold and it rained
and we were dark and worried.
We moved from sun to shade
and back again.
Look, that was once us
sailing down the small
sand hill to the beach
with you in our arms.

Notes

"Coming Upon a Crab in the Sand" is inspired by William
Shakespeare's sonnet 108, "What's in the brain that ink may
character."

"Portrait of a Lady" is for Lelia Ruckenstein and is inspired by
The Portrait of a Lady by Henry James. The italic lines in the
poem are direct quotations from the novel.

"April Mornings" is after Robert Hayden's "Sunday Mornings."

Acknowledgments

The American Scholar: "1. Chatter," "2. Manhood," "4. The Pack," "5. Mind Game," "8. The Mothers," "9. The Fathers," "13. The Players"

Virginia Quarterly Review: "3. The Hotdog," "6. The Girls," "11. The Pillage"

The Chronicle of Higher Education: "Driving Lesson" (as "Teaching My Son to Drive")

The Kenyon Review: "The Lucky Ones," "Jane Austen"

The New Yorker: "12. The Dugout"

The Yale Review: "Sonnet for the Misbegotten"

Harvard Review: "Daylight Savings," "Prophesy"

Ohio Poem in Your Pocket Day: "Tree"

The New Republic: "After the Storm"

The Atlantic: "American Pastoral"

The New York Times Magazine: "Marriage Nests"

Poem-a-Day, published by the Academy of American Poets: "Morning Nocturne"

The Gettysburg Review: "Coming Upon a Crab in the Sand," "Pilgrims," "The Guardians: Last Notes"

Special thanks to Deborah Garrison, Sarah Chalfant, Jin Auh, Eavan Boland, Kimiko Hahn, and David Baker.

A NOTE ABOUT THE AUTHOR

Jill Bialosky was born in Cleveland, Ohio. She received her Bachelor of Arts at Ohio University (1979), received a Master of Arts from The Johns Hopkins University (1980), and a Master of Fine Arts from the University of Iowa's Writers' Workshop (1983). She is the author of three poetry collections: *The End of Desire,* Alfred A. Knopf, 1997; *Subterranean,* Alfred A. Knopf, 2001, a finalist for the James Laughlin Award from the Academy of American Poets; and *Intruder,* Alfred A. Knopf, 2008, finalist for the 2009 Paterson Poetry Prize. *The Skiers: Selected Poems,* Arc Publications, was published in the UK in 2009. She is the author of two novels, *House Under Snow,* 2002 (Harcourt), and *The Life Room,* 2007 (Harcourt), and a memoir, *History of a Suicide,* 2011 (Atria). It was a *New York Times* bestseller and finalist for a Books for a Better Life Award and a finalist for the Ohioana Book Award in nonfiction. She co-edited with Helen Schulman *Wanting a Child,* Farrar, Straus & Giroux, 1998. Bialosky's poems and essays have been published in many magazines, among them *The New Yorker, O, The Oprah Magazine, Real Simple, The Nation, The Atlantic Monthly, Redbook, The Kenyon Review, Harvard Review, The Antioch Review, The New Republic, The Paris Review, Poetry, The American Poetry Review,* and *The Yale Review.*

A NOTE ON THE TYPE

The text of this book was set in Bembo, a facsimile of a typeface cut by Francesco Griffo for Aldus Manutius, the celebrated Venetian printer, in 1495. The face was named for Pietro Cardinal Bembo, the author of the small treatise entitled *De Aetna* in which it first appeared. Through the research of Stanley Morison, it is now generally acknowledged that all oldstyle type designs up to the time of William Caslon can be traced to the Bembo cut. The present-day version of Bembo was introduced by the Monotype Corporation of London in 1929. Sturdy, well-balanced, and finely proportioned, Bembo is a face of rare beauty and great legibility in all of its sizes.

Composed by North Market Street Graphics,
Lancaster, Pennsylvania

Printed and bound by Thomson-Shore,
Dexter, Michigan

Designed by Soonyoung Kwon